Making
DREAM ICE CREAM

Making
DREAM ICE CREAM
Easy ices and sorbets for every season

HH
HERMES
HOUSE

This edition published by Hermes House
27 West 20th Street, New York, NY 10011

HERMES HOUSE books are available for bulk purchase
for sales promotion and for premium use. For details, write or call
the sales director, Hermes House, 27 West 20th Street, New York,
NY 10011; (800) 354-9657

Hermes House is an imprint of Anness Publishing Inc.

ISBN 1-84038-239-2

Publisher Joanna Lorenz
Series Editor Sarah Ainley
Copy Editor Jenni Fleetwood
Designers Patrick McLeavey & Partners
Illustrator Anna Koska
Photographers Edward Allwright, James Duncan, Michelle Garrett,
Amanda Heywood & Don Last
Recipes Jacqueline Clark, Carole Clements,
Joanna Farrow, Rafi Fernandez, Christine France, Ruby Le Bois
and Elizabeth Wolf-Cohen

Printed and bound in Singapore

© Anness Publishing Limited 1998
Updated © 1999
1 3 5 7 9 10 8 6 4 2

Contents

Introduction

It is thought that ices and ice creams originated in China. The recipes were copied by the early traders and transported to the Mediterranean, where they  were perfected by great cooks like those who catered for the Medici family in Italy. Florentine banquets were famous for the range of iced desserts that graced the tables – different flavours were presented every day – and it was not long before all of Europe echoed to the popular cry of the ice cream vendor.

In India, cooks prepared kulfi, a delicately spiced pistachio ice cream, while in Egypt, it was fresh mango that formed the basis of what many believe to be the most delicious ice cream of all.

It is Thomas Jefferson who is credited with introducing ice cream to the United States. The concoction drew gasps when it first appeared at a state dinner at the White House, and today ice cream remains America's most popular dessert, available in an astonishing array of flavours and forms.

Ice cream was originally just what it sounds like – a flavoured cream packed in a container, surrounded by a mixture of salt and ice, and churned until frozen by the action of a paddle that was cranked by hand. When the domestic freezer was invented, salt and ice were no longer required, but the mixture still needed to be whisked frequently as it froze, to break down ice crystals as they formed. This method of manufacture was more efficient, but the results were not as good as when ice cream had been constantly cranked. The increasing demand for this delightful dessert meant that it would only be a matter of time before the mechanical ice cream maker was developed to solve the problem.

Of the ice cream makers available today, some operate in the freezer, while others are free-standing appliances, consisting of a bowl pre-frozen before the ice cream is added and churned by a paddle in the lid. Freezing is rapid and the results are excellent. The most sophisticated free-standing model has its own freezer unit – all you do is add the ingredients to the bowl, switch on and serve the ice cream twenty minutes later.

Making your own ice cream means that you control the ingredients – and the cost. Yogurt, buttermilk or fromage frais will make lower-calorie versions, liqueurs can be

added to please dinner party guests and fruit purées can be transformed into luscious sorbets.

Ice cream desserts can be as simple or as elaborate as you like. After a rich meal, serve a simple water-ice or a granita. Parties call for sumptuous parfaits – ice cream or whipped cream layered in a tall glass with chocolate or fruit, and then frozen – or sundaes, which are assembled at the last minute. The bombe is another brilliant invention: pack two ice creams into a mould and freeze. The result is a dessert that looks and tastes fantastic.

If you've never made your own ice cream, now is the time to try. It isn't difficult – just follow the easy recipes in this collection and you'll soon have it licked!

Simple Sauces

APRICOT

Heat 225g/8oz/¾ cup apricot jam with 60ml/4 tbsp water. Allow to boil for 10 minutes, stirring continuously, then press through a sieve into a heatproof bowl. Stir in lemon juice to taste, and add a little orange-flavoured liqueur, if you like. Serve the sauce warm, poured over ice cream.

BUTTERSCOTCH

Melt 50g/2oz/¼ cup butter with 115g/4oz/½ cup demerara sugar and 50g/2oz/3 tbsp golden syrup in a heavy-based saucepan over a medium heat. Bring the mixture to the boil, stirring constantly, then cook over a gentle heat until golden brown. Serve the sauce hot, over ice cream.

CHOCOLATE

Gently heat 150ml/¼ pint/⅔ cup double cream with 50g/2oz/4 tbsp diced butter and 50g/2oz/¼ cup caster sugar in a large saucepan, stirring, until smooth. Allow to cool, then stir in 175g/6oz/1 cup chocolate chips or plain chocolate, broken into chunks, until melted. Serve hot. For a variation use 175g/6oz white chocolate.

RASPBERRY

Purée 225g/8oz/1¼ cups raspberries with 50g/2oz/½ cup icing sugar and 30ml/2 tbsp orange juice in a blender or food processor. Press through a fine sieve into a bowl to remove the seeds. Stir in a splash of framboise syrup if you like. Serve the sauce drizzled over ice cream.

LEMON & LIME

Peel the rind from 1 lemon and 2 limes and squeeze the juice from the fruit. Place the rind in a saucepan, cover with water and bring to the boil. Drain through a sieve and reserve the rind. Mix 50g/2 oz/¼ cup caster sugar in a bowl with 25ml/1½ tbsp arrowroot, and add a little water to give a smooth paste. Heat 175ml/6 fl oz/¾ cup water, pour in the arrowroot, and stir until the sauce boils and thickens. Stir in 15ml/1 tbsp sugar, citrus juice and reserved rind, and serve hot. Sprinkle the dessert with fresh mint, to decorate.

Dreamy Decorations

CHOCOLATE CARAQUE

Spread melted chocolate over a cool, smooth work surface. When it is just set, pull the broad blade of a cook's knife across the surface at an angle of 45° to form quill-like chocolate shavings.

CHOCOLATE LEAVES

Paint the undersides of clean, dry rose leaves with melted chocolate. Leave to set, chocolate side up, on non-stick baking paper, then peel away the rose leaves to reveal the chocolate leaves.

FROSTED FRUIT

Have ready tiny bunches of grapes or black-currants, or stemmed cherries. Brush the fruits with water, then roll or dip them into caster sugar to coat. Allow to dry completely before using as a decoration.

ROSE PETALS

Exotic desserts like Turkish Delight Ice Cream look lovely with a scattering of rose petals. Tiny rosebuds can be frosted: brush them lightly with egg white, then dip them in caster sugar and allow to dry before use.

TOASTED ALMONDS

Spread flaked almonds in a single layer in a grill pan. Grill under a medium heat until the nuts turn golden brown. Shake the pan often and watch the nuts all the time as they burn very easily.

SUNDAE BEST

You can really go to town when it comes to decorating a sundae. Marshmallows, fan wafers, chocolate flake bars and glacé fruits all go down well.

CITRUS RIND

Top citrus sorbets with thinly pared orange, lemon or lime rind. Be sure to avoid the bitter white pith when you pare the fruit. Blanch the rind in boiling water, then drain and dry it before use.

9

Techniques

PREPARING SYRUP FOR A SORBET

Water ices and sorbets start with a simple syrup. Heat the sugar and water in a heavy-based saucepan over a medium heat, stirring gently until all the sugar is dissolved. Bring to the boil and boil without stirring for 2 minutes or for the time stated in the recipe.

WHISKING EGG WHITES

Sorbets are lightened by the addition of whisked egg whites. Use a completely clean, grease-free bowl and beat the whites with a whisk or electric mixer until stiff and glossy.

COOKED FRUIT PUREE

Fruit purées are a useful base for sorbets and dessert sauces. Cook the fruit with a small amount of sugar (and water, if needed) until the fruit is tender and the sugar has dissolved. Remove any stones from the fruit, then purée it in a blender or food processor.

STRAINING FRUIT

Many recipes call for fruit to be strained, to remove the stones and skin. Firm fruits, such as apples, should be cooked and puréed before you strain them. Pour the purée into a sieve over a large bowl, then use a wooden spoon to firmly press the purée through the sieve. Soft fruits, like raspberries, can be strained raw, and spooned directly onto the serving plate.

10

MAKING AN ICE BOWL

Ice creams and sorbets look spectacular in an ice bowl. Choose two freezerproof bowls, one about 7.5cm/3in wider than the other. Pour cold water into the larger bowl to two thirds full, then centre the smaller bowl in the water, weighting it so that it floats level with the big bowl. Keep it in place with masking tape. Top up the surrounding water if necessary, then freeze, adding flowers or leaves when the water is semi-frozen, if liked. Ease out the small bowl when frozen, release the ice bowl and store in the freezer until needed.

TIPS FOR PERFECT ICES

- *The faster you freeze ice cream, the fewer ice crystals will form, so turn the freezer to the coldest setting 1 hour before, or use the fast-freeze facility.*

- *Don't make too much at one time. Not only will this take too long, but it will result in the formation of larger ice crystals.*

- *Constant churning in an ice-cream maker gives the creamiest results, but whisking by hand when ice crystals start to form, then once or twice more during freezing, is perfectly adequate.*

- *Home-made ice cream freezes hard. Allow it to soften slightly before serving. This not only makes it easier to scoop but also gives the flavours a chance to "ripen".*

- *Add chunky flavourings, like chopped preserved ginger, nuts or chocolate chips, when the ice cream is partially frozen, or they will sink.*

- *Use a scoop or baller dipped in lukewarm water for shaping ice cream, or make simple ovals between two dessert spoons.*

Classic
Ice Creams

Vanilla Ice Cream

INGREDIENTS

300ml/10fl oz/1¼ cups double cream
1 vanilla pod or 2.5ml/½ tsp vanilla essence
2 eggs, lightly beaten
50g/2oz/¼ cup caster sugar
blackberry sauce, to serve (optional)

SERVES 4

1 Pour the cream into a heavy-based saucepan. Add the vanilla pod, if using. Bring the mixture to just below boiling point. Remove the vanilla pod.

2 Place the eggs and sugar in a heat-proof bowl. Set the bowl over a pan of barely simmering water and whisk until the mixture is pale and thick. Whisking vigorously, pour in the cream in a steady stream. Continue to whisk the mixture just until it begins to thicken.

3 Whisk in the vanilla essence, if using. Cool, then spoon into a suitable container for freezing. Freeze until crystals form around the edges, whisk until smooth, then freeze again.

13

4 Repeat the process once or twice, then freeze the mixture until firm. Alternatively, use an ice cream maker, following the manufacturer's instructions. Allow the ice cream to soften slightly before serving in scoops, with a fruit sauce, if liked.

VARIATION

Make a less rich version of the ice cream by substituting buttermilk for three-quarters of the double cream, and using 30ml/2 tbsp clear honey instead of the sugar.

Chocolate Ice Cream

INGREDIENTS

225g/8oz plain chocolate, broken into squares
750ml/1¼ pints/3 cups milk
1 vanilla pod
4 egg yolks
115g/4oz/½ cup granulated sugar

SERVES 4–6

1 Half fill a saucepan with water, allow to boil, then remove from the heat. Place the chocolate in a heatproof bowl over the pan. Set aside until the chocolate has melted, stirring occasionally.

2 Pour the milk into a heavy-based saucepan. Add the vanilla pod. Keeping the heat fairly low, bring the mixture to just below boiling point. Remove the vanilla pod.

3 Place the egg yolks in a large heatproof bowl and whisk in the sugar. Whisk in the hot milk, then add the melted chocolate. Place the bowl over a pan of barely simmering water and stir until the chocolate custard thickens slightly. Allow to cool.

4 Spoon the mixture into a suitable container for freezing. Freeze until ice crystals form around the edges of the container, then process or beat the mixture until smooth. Repeat the process once or twice, then freeze the mixture until firm. Alternatively, use an ice cream maker, following the manufacturer's instructions. Allow the ice cream to soften slightly before serving it in scoops.

14

Hazelnut Ice Cream

INGREDIENTS

75g / 3oz / ¾ cup hazelnuts
75g / 3oz / 6 tbsp granulated sugar
475ml / 16fl oz / 2 cups milk
1 vanilla pod
4 egg yolks

SERVES 4–6

1 Spread the hazelnuts on a baking sheet. Place under a medium grill for about 5 minutes, shaking the sheet often, until the nuts are toasted. Allow them to cool slightly, then rub off the outer skins with a clean dish towel. Chop very finely or grind in a food processor or nut mill, with 30ml/2 tbsp of the sugar.

2 Pour the milk into a heavy-based saucepan. Add the vanilla pod and bring the mixture to just below boiling point. Remove the vanilla pod.

3 Place the egg yolks in a heatproof bowl. Whisk in the remaining sugar, then the hot milk. Place the bowl over a pan of barely simmering water and stir in the ground hazelnuts. Stir until the custard thickens slightly, then allow to cool.

4 Spoon the mixture into a suitable container for freezing. Freeze until ice crystals form around the edges, then process or beat the mixture until smooth. Repeat  the process twice, then freeze until the mixture is firm. Alternatively, use an ice cream maker, following the manufacturer's instructions. Allow the ice cream to soften slightly before serving it in scoops.

15

Brown Bread Ice Cream

INGREDIENTS

*50g/2oz/½ cup hazelnuts, toasted and ground
(see Hazelnut Ice Cream)
75g/3oz/1½ cups fresh wholemeal breadcrumbs
50g/2oz/⅓ cup demerara sugar
3 egg whites
115g/4oz/½ cup caster sugar
300ml/½ pint/1¼ cups double cream
few drops of vanilla essence
fresh mint sprigs, to decorate
SAUCE
225g/8oz/1½ cups blackcurrants, thawed
if frozen
75g/3oz/6 tbsp caster sugar
15ml/1 tbsp crème de cassis*

SERVES 6

16

2 Whisk the egg whites in a grease-free bowl until stiff peaks form, then gradually whisk in the sugar until thick and glossy. Whip the cream to soft peaks; fold it into the meringue with the breadcrumb mixture and vanilla essence. Spoon the mixture into a 1.2 litre/2 pint/5 cup loaf tin. Level the surface, then cover and freeze until firm.

3 Meanwhile make the sauce. Put the blackcurrants in a bowl with the sugar. Toss gently, cover and leave for 30 minutes, then purée in a blender or food processor. Press through a nylon sieve into a bowl, stir in the crème de cassis and chill well. Serve the ice cream in slices, with the sauce. Decorate with the fresh mint sprigs.

1 Spread out the ground hazelnuts and breadcrumbs on a baking sheet. Sprinkle over the demerara sugar. Grill the hazelnuts under a medium heat until the mixture is crisp and browned. Leave to cool.

Kulfi

INGREDIENTS

3 x 400ml / 14fl oz cans evaporated milk
3 egg whites
350g / 12oz / 2⅔ cups icing sugar
5ml / 1 tsp ground cardamom
15ml / 1 tbsp rosewater
175g / 6oz / 1½ cups pistachio nuts, chopped
75g / 3oz / ¾ cup flaked almonds
75g / 3oz / ½ cup sultanas
25g / 1oz / 3 tbsp glacé cherries, halved

SERVES 4–6

1 Remove the labels from the cans of evaporated milk and lay them on their sides in a saucepan with a tight-fitting lid. Pour in water to come three-quarters of the way up the cans. Bring to the boil, lower the heat, cover and simmer for 20 minutes. Let the unopened cans cool in the water, then remove and place in the fridge for 24 hours.

17

2 Whisk the egg whites in a grease-free bowl until stiff peaks form. Open the cans and pour the milk into a chilled bowl. Whisk until doubled in bulk, then fold in the egg whites and icing sugar.

3 Gently fold in the ground cardamom, rosewater, nuts, sultanas and cherries. Cover the bowl and freeze until ice crystals form around the edges, then mix  well with a fork. Return to the freezer and freeze again until firm. Allow the kulfi to soften slightly before serving it in scoops.

Turkish Delight Ice Cream

INGREDIENTS

300ml / ½ pint / 1¼ cups milk
4 egg yolks
115g / 4oz / ½ cup caster sugar
175g / 6oz / 1 cup rose-flavoured Turkish
delight, chopped
30–45ml / 2–3 tbsp water
15ml / 1 tbsp rosewater
300ml / ½ pint / 1¼ cups double cream
thin almond biscuits, to serve (optional)

SERVES 6

18

1 Bring the milk to the boil in a large heavy-based pan. Whisk the egg yolks with the caster sugar in a heatproof bowl. Then whisk in the hot milk.

2 Place the bowl over a pan of barely simmering water and stir until the custard thickens slightly. Remove from the heat, cover the surface of the custard closely with greaseproof paper (to prevent the formation of a skin) and allow to cool.

3 Meanwhile, heat the Turkish delight and water in a small pan. When most of the mixture has melted, and only a few lumps remain, stir it into the cold custard, with the rosewater and cream.

4 Spoon the mixture into a suitable container for freezing. Freeze until ice crystals form around the edges, then tip into a bowl and whisk the mixture well.

Return to the freezer container. Repeat the process once or twice, then freeze until firm. Alternatively, use an ice cream maker, following the manufacturer's instructions. Allow the ice cream to soften slightly before serving it in small scoops with the thin almond biscuits, if using.

COOK'S TIP

This ice cream will look extra special decorated
with a scattering of pink rose petals, if you have any.

Pineapple Ice Cream

INGREDIENTS

600ml / 1 pint / 2½ cups whipping cream
25g / 1oz / 4 tbsp icing sugar
8 eggs, separated
115g / 4oz / ½ cup caster sugar
2.5ml / ½ tsp vanilla essence
425g / 15oz can pineapple chunks, very
finely chopped
75g / 3oz / ¾ cup pistachio nuts, chopped
wafer biscuits, to serve

SERVES 8–10

20

1 Whip the cream with the icing sugar in a bowl until soft peaks form. Place the egg yolks, sugar and vanilla essence in a second bowl. Beat until the mixture is thick and pale, then fold in the whipped cream.

2 Whisk the egg whites in a grease-free bowl until stiff peaks form. Using a metal spoon, fold the egg whites gently but thoroughly into the cream mixture.

3 Then stir in the chopped pineapple and pistachios until well distributed. Spoon the mixture into a suitable container for freezing. Freeze until ice crystals

form around the edges, then beat the mixture until smooth. Repeat the process once or twice, then freeze until firm. Alternatively, use an ice cream maker, following the manufacturer's instructions. Allow the ice cream to soften before scooping it into dessert dishes. Serve with wafer biscuits.

Coconut Ice Cream

INGREDIENTS

400g/14oz can evaporated milk
400g/14oz can condensed milk
400g/14oz can coconut milk
5ml/1 tsp grated nutmeg
5ml/1 tsp almond essence
lemon balm sprigs, lime slices and shredded
coconut, to decorate

SERVES 8

1 Mix the evaporated milk, condensed milk and coconut milk in a large bowl which will fit in the freezer. Stir in the nutmeg and almond essence.

2 Freeze until ice crystals begin to form around the edges of the mixture, then remove from the freezer and whisk by hand or with a hand-held mixer until the mixture is fluffy and has almost doubled in bulk.

3 Tip the mixture into a suitable container for freezing, cover and freeze until solid. Allow the ice cream to soften slightly before serving in scoops, decorated with lemon balm sprigs, lime slices and the shredded coconut.

Summer Fruit Salad Ice Cream

INGREDIENTS

900g / 2lb / 5 cups mixed soft summer fruit
(such as raspberries, strawberries,
blackcurrants, redcurrants)
175ml / 6fl oz / ¾ cup red grape juice
15ml / 1 tbsp powdered gelatine
2 eggs, separated
250ml / 8fl oz / 1 cup natural yogurt

SERVES 6

22

1 Set half the fruit aside for the decoration. Purée the rest in a blender or food processor, then rub through a sieve into a bowl, to remove any seeds.

2 Heat the grape juice in a small pan until just below boiling point. Remove from the heat and sprinkle the gelatine over the surface. Stir the grape juice to dissolve the gelatine completely. Cool slightly.

3 Whisk the egg yolks, yogurt and dissolved gelatine into the fruit purée. Pour into a suitable container for freezing. Freeze until crystals form around the edges and the mixture is slushy.

4 Whisk the egg whites in a grease-free bowl until stiff peaks form. Tip the half-frozen yogurt ice cream into a bowl and quickly fold in the egg whites.

5 Return the mixture to the freezer container and freeze until solid. Soften slightly before serving in scoops, with the reserved soft fruits.

COOK'S TIP
Hull the fruit used for the purée, but leave the rest whole — attached to the stalks — for the decoration.

Mint Ice Cream

INGREDIENTS

600ml / 1 pint / 2½ cups single cream
1 vanilla pod or 2.5ml / ½ tsp vanilla essence
8 egg yolks
75g / 3oz / 6 tbsp caster sugar
60ml / 4 tbsp finely chopped fresh mint
fresh mint sprigs, to decorate

SERVES 8

24

1 Pour the cream into a heavy-based saucepan. Add the vanilla pod, if using. Keeping the heat fairly low, bring the mixture to just below boiling point. Remove the vanilla pod.

2 Place the egg yolks and sugar in a large mixing bowl. Beat until the mixture is pale and light, using a balloon whisk or an electric beater. Transfer to a pan.

3 Whisking vigorously, pour the hot cream into the saucepan in a steady stream. Continue to whisk until the mixture thickens slightly. Whisk in the vanilla essence, if using. Leave to cool.

4 Stir in the mint. Spoon the mixture into a suitable container for freezing. Freeze until ice crystals form around the edges, then beat the mixture until smooth.

5 Repeat the process once or twice, then freeze until firm. Alternatively, use an ice cream maker, following the manufacturer's instructions. Allow the ice cream to stand at room temperature for 15 minutes before serving, to soften slightly. This ice cream looks spectacular scooped into an ice bowl, decorated with the fresh mint sprigs.

Rocky Road Ice Cream

INGREDIENTS

115g/4oz plain chocolate, broken into squares
150ml/¼ pint/⅔ cup milk
300ml/½ pint/1¼ cups double cream
*115g/4oz/1½ cups marshmallows,
chopped if large*
50g/2oz/½ cup glacé cherries, chopped
50g/2oz/½ cup crumbled shortbread biscuits
30ml/2 tbsp chopped walnuts

SERVES 6

26

1 Melt the squares of chocolate in the milk in a large saucepan over a gentle heat, stirring from time to time. Allow the chocolate milk to cool completely.

2 Whip the cream in a bowl until it just holds its shape. Beat in the chocolate milk, then tip the mixture into a suitable container for freezing. Freeze until ice crystals form around the edges. Alternatively, churn the mixture in an ice cream maker until it is thick and almost frozen.

3 Using a spatula, stir the marshmallows, chopped glacé cherries, crumbled biscuits and walnuts into the iced mixture. Freeze again until it is firm. Allow the ice cream to soften slightly before serving it in scoops or slices.

COOK'S TIP
Use kitchen scissors to chop the marshmallows, dipping the blades in a jug of boiling water between snips.

Coffee Ice Cream with Caramelized Pecans

INGREDIENTS

300ml / ½ pint / 1¼ cups milk
15ml / 1 tbsp demerara sugar
15ml / 1 tbsp instant coffee granules
1 egg, plus 2 yolks
300ml / ½ pint / 1¼ cups double cream
15ml / 1 tbsp caster sugar
CARAMELIZED PECANS
115g / 4oz / 1 cup pecan nut halves
50g / 2oz / ⅓ cup soft dark brown sugar
30ml / 2 tbsp water

SERVES 4–6

1 Heat the milk and demerara sugar in a heavy-based saucepan, stirring until the sugar dissolves. Bring to the boil, remove from the heat and stir in the instant coffee until dissolved.

2 Combine the egg and extra yolks in a heatproof bowl. Set the bowl over a saucepan of barely simmering water and whisk until the eggs are pale and thick. Remove from the heat.

3 Whisking vigorously, pour in the coffee-flavoured milk in a steady stream. Replace over the water and stir until the custard thickens slightly. Leave the mixture to cool.

4 Whip the cream with the caster sugar until soft peaks form. Fold it into the coffee custard, then tip the mixture into a suitable container for freezing. Freeze until ice crystals form around the edges, then beat the mixture until smooth. Repeat the process once or twice, then freeze until firm. Alternatively, use an ice cream maker, following the manufacturer's instructions.

5 Caramelize the pecans. Preheat the oven to 180°C/350°F/Gas 4. Spread the nuts in a single layer on a baking sheet. Bake for 10–15 minutes, checking frequently, until they are roasted.

6 Next, dissolve the brown sugar in the water over a low heat, then bring to the boil. When the mixture bubbles and begins to turn golden, tip in the  roasted pecans. Cook for 1–2 minutes over a medium heat until the pecans are well coated.

7 Spread the pecan nuts on a lightly oiled baking sheet and set aside until they have cooled. Allow the ice cream to soften slightly at room temperature before serving it in scoops, with the caramelized pecans.

28

Sorbets & Ices

Mango Sorbet with Mango Sauce

INGREDIENTS

2 x 400g/14oz cans sliced mangoes, drained
2.5ml/½ tsp lemon juice
grated rind of 1 orange and 1 lemon
4 egg whites
50g/2oz/¼ cup caster sugar
120ml/4fl oz/½ cup double cream
50g/2oz/½ cup icing sugar

SERVES 4–6

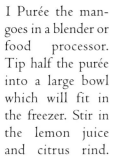

1 Purée the mangoes in a blender or food processor. Tip half the purée into a large bowl which will fit in the freezer. Stir in the lemon juice and citrus rind. Reserve the remaining purée for the sauce.

2 Whisk the egg whites in a grease-free bowl until stiff peaks form, then gradually whisk in the caster sugar until thick and glossy. Fold into the mango purée and freeze until ice crystals form around the edges of the bowl.

3 Beat the mixture until it is smooth, then scrape into a freezer container and freeze until firm.

4 Make the mango sauce. Whip the double cream with the icing sugar until soft peaks form, then fold in the reserved mango purée. Spoon into a serving bowl, then cover the bowl and chill for 24 hours.

5 Allow the sorbet to soften for about 10 minutes before serving in scoops, topped with the sauce.

Watermelon Sorbet

INGREDIENTS

1kg / 2¼lb piece of watermelon
225g / 8oz / 1 cup caster sugar
juice of 1 lemon
120ml / 4fl oz / ½ cup water
2 egg whites
fresh mint leaves, to decorate

SERVES 6

1 Cut the watermelon into cubes, discarding the peel and any seeds. Mash a quarter of the cubes in a shallow bowl. Purée the remaining watermelon in a blender or food processor, in batches if necessary.

2 Mix the sugar, lemon juice and water in a saucepan. Stir over a low heat until the sugar dissolves, then boil, without stirring, for 2 minutes. Tip into a large bowl and stir in the watermelon purée and the mashed watermelon. Cool, then pour the mixture into a suitable container for freezing.

3 Freeze until ice crystals form around the edges of the mixture, then scrape it into a bowl and beat until smooth. Freeze the mixture as before, then beat and freeze again.

4 In a grease-free bowl, whisk the egg whites until they form soft peaks. Beat the iced mixture again, then fold in the egg whites. Return the sorbet to the freezer container, freeze for 1 hour, then beat again and freeze until firm. Allow the sorbet to soften before serving in scoops, decorated with the fresh mint leaves.

Blackcurrant Sorbet

INGREDIENTS

500g / 1¼lb blackcurrants
115g / 4oz / ½ cup caster sugar
120ml / 4fl oz / ½ cup water
15ml / 1 tbsp egg white
fresh mint sprigs, to decorate

SERVES 4

1 Strip the blackcurrants from their stalks by pulling them through the tines of a fork. Mix the sugar and water in a saucepan. Stir over a low heat until the sugar dissolves, then boil, without stirring, for 2 minutes.

2 Purée the blackcurrants with the lemon juice in a blender or food processor. Add the sugar syrup and process briefly to mix. Press the mixture through a sieve set over a bowl, to remove any seeds.

3 Pour the blackcurrant purée into a non-metallic container suitable for use in the freezer. Cover and freeze until ice crystals form around the edges and the mixture is slushy.

4 Scrape spoonfuls of sorbet into a blender or food processor. Process until smooth, then, with the motor running, add the egg white and process until well mixed.

5 Tip the sorbet back into the freezer container and freeze until almost firm. Process again. Serve immediately or return to the freezer until solid, in which case the sorbet should be allowed to soften slightly before serving. Serve in scoops, decorated with the fresh mint sprigs.

33

Chocolate Sorbet with Red Fruits

INGREDIENTS

475ml/16fl oz/2 cups water
45ml/3 tbsp clear honey
115g/4oz/½ cup caster sugar
75g/3oz/¾ cup cocoa powder
50g/2oz plain chocolate, broken into squares
400g/14oz/3 cups soft red fruits (such as raspberries, strawberries, redcurrants), to serve

SERVES 6

34

1 Mix the water, honey and caster sugar in a large saucepan. Gradually add the cocoa powder, and stir continuously until the liquid is smooth. Cook

gently over a low heat, stirring occasionally, until the sugar and cocoa have dissolved completely.

2 Remove the saucepan from the heat, add the chocolate, a few squares at a time, and stir until melted. Set the saucepan aside until the mixture has cooled.

3 For a really fine texture, churn the mixture in an ice cream maker until it has completely frozen. Alternatively, pour the mixture into a container suitable for use in the freezer, freeze until slushy, then whisk until smooth and freeze again. Whisk for a second time before the mixture hardens completely.

4 Allow the sorbet to soften slightly at room temperature before serving in scoops or ovals, decorated with the soft berry fruits.

COOK'S TIP

To shape the sorbet into ovals, use two tablespoons. Scoop out the sorbet with one tablespoon, then use the other to smooth it off and transfer it to a plate.

Iced Oranges

INGREDIENTS

150g / 5oz / ⅔ cup granulated sugar
120ml / 4fl oz / ½ cup water
juice of 1 lemon
14 medium oranges
8 fresh bay leaves, to decorate

SERVES 8

1 Mix the sugar, water and half the lemon juice in a heavy-based saucepan. Stir over a low heat until the sugar dissolves, then boil, without stirring, for 2 minutes. Set the syrup aside to cool.

2 Choose eight oranges of similar size to use as containers for the sorbet. Slice off their tops to make lids, and take a slim slice off the bottom of each so that they stand upright. Carefully scoop the flesh into a bowl, keeping the orange shells intact, and set aside. Put the orange shells and lids on a baking sheet and place in the freezer.

3 Grate the rind from two of the remaining oranges. Squeeze all of them into a measuring jug, then add any juice from the reserved flesh. Pour in water or bought orange juice, if necessary, to make this liquid up to 750ml / 1¼ pints / 3 cups. Stir in the grated orange rind, syrup and remaining lemon juice. Pour into a shallow freezer container and freeze until ice crystals form around the edges and the mixture is slushy.

4 Scrape the mixture into a bowl and whisk until smooth. Freeze again, until firm but not solid. Pack the sorbet in the orange shells, mounding it up, and set the lids on top. Freeze until ready to serve. When serving, decorate the lids by making a hole in each with a skewer, then pushing in a bay leaf.

36

Lime & Mango Sorbet in Lime Shells

INGREDIENTS

4 large limes
7.5ml / 1½ tsp powdered gelatine
1 ripe mango, peeled and chopped
2 egg whites
15ml / 1 tbsp caster sugar
pared lime rind strips, to decorate

SERVES 4

1 Slice the tops off the limes, and take a slim slice off the bottom of each so that they stand upright. Carefully scoop the flesh into a bowl, keeping the lime shells intact. Squeeze out all the juice from the lime flesh and put 45ml/3 tbsp of it in a small heatproof bowl. Sprinkle the gelatine on top and leave until spongy.

2 Purée the mango with the remaining lime juice (about 30ml/2 tbsp) in a blender or food processor. Place the heatproof bowl over a small pan of hot water and stir until the gelatine has dissolved completely. Add it to the mango purée and process briefly to mix.

3 Whisk the egg whites in a grease-free bowl until they form soft peaks. Whisk in the caster sugar, then fold into the mango mixture. Spoon into the lime shells, mounding the mixture. Freeze any excess sorbet in ramekin dishes.

4 Freeze the filled shells until firm, wrap them in clear film and replace them in the freezer. Before serving, unwrap the limes and allow the sorbet to soften slightly. Decorate with the lime rind strips.

Rhubarb & Orange Water-ice

INGREDIENTS

350g/12oz pink rhubarb
grated rind and juice of 1 medium orange
30ml/2 tbsp clear honey
5ml/1 tsp powdered gelatine
quartered orange slices, to decorate

SERVES 4

3 Heat the remaining orange juice, then remove from the heat. Stir in the gelatine until it has completely dissolved, then stir the liquid into the rhubarb, and add the remaining orange rind.

4 Tip the mixture into a suitable container for freezing. Freeze until ice crystals form around the edges and the mixture is slushy.

5 Scrape the mixture into a bowl and beat until smooth. Return it to the freezer and freeze until firm. Allow the water-ice to soften slightly before serving it in scoops, decorated with quartered orange slices.

1 Trim the rhubarb and slice it into 2.5cm/1in lengths. If you have not been able to obtain pink (forced) rhubarb, and the stems are a bit stringy, peel them thinly before slicing.

2 Put the rhubarb into a saucepan and add half the orange rind and juice. Bring to simmering point and cook over a very low heat until the rhubarb is just tender. Stir in the honey.

COOK'S TIP
Pink (forced) rhubarb is naturally quite sweet,
but you may find it necessary to add a little more
honey – or caster sugar – to the mixture.

Speciality
Iced Desserts

Fried Wontons & Ice Cream

INGREDIENTS

oil, for deep frying
12 wonton wrappers
8 scoops of your favourite ice cream (or
4 scoops each of two varieties)

SERVES 4

1 Heat the oil in a deep-fryer or large saucepan to 180°C/350°F or until a cube of dried bread browns in 30–45 seconds.

2 Add a few wonton wrappers at a time, so that they do not crowd the pan too much. Fry for 1–2 minutes on each side, until the wrappers are crisp and light golden brown. Lift out and drain on kitchen paper.

3 To serve, place one wonton on each plate. Top with a scoop of ice cream, then add a second wonton and a second scoop of ice cream. Finish with a final wonton. Serve at once.

41

COOK'S TIP

Mix and match the scoops of ice cream to contrast the colours but take care to choose complementary flavours. Try coffee with hazelnut, Turkish delight with vanilla or chocolate with mint.

Praline Ice Cream in Baskets

INGREDIENTS

50g / 2oz / ½ cup blanched almonds
60ml / 4 tbsp water
175g / 6oz / ¾ cup caster sugar
475ml / 16fl oz / 2 cups milk
6 egg yolks
250ml / 8fl oz / 1 cup double cream
8 biscuit baskets, to serve

SERVES 6–8

42

2 Break the nut praline into small pieces. Grind in a food processor until fine. Then, in a large saucepan, bring the milk to just below boiling point.

1 Brush a baking sheet lightly with oil. Mix the nuts, water and 65g/ 2½oz/5 tbsp of the sugar in a saucepan. Stir over a low heat until the sugar dissolves, then boil, without stirring, until the syrup is a medium caramel colour and the nuts begin to pop. Carefully pour the nuts on to the baking sheet and set aside until cold.

3 Whisk the egg yolks and remaining sugar in a heatproof bowl until pale and thick. Whisk in the hot milk, then place the bowl over a pan of simmering water and stir until the mixture thickens. Remove the bowl from the heat and stir in the double cream. Set aside to cool.

4 Stir the praline into the mixture, reserving 30ml/2 tbsp for decoration. Churn in an ice cream maker until frozen. Alternatively, pour it into a freezer container, freeze until slushy, whisk until smooth, then freeze again. Whisk for a second time before the mixture hardens completely.

5 Allow the ice cream to soften before serving, in the baskets, sprinkled with the reserved praline.

Frozen Apple & Blackberry Terrine

INGREDIENTS

450g/1lb cooking apples
300ml/½ pint/1¼ cups apple juice
15ml/1 tbsp clear honey
5ml/1 tsp vanilla essence
350g/12oz/2 cups fresh or thawed frozen blackberries
15ml/1 tbsp powdered gelatine
2 egg whites
fresh apple slices and blackberries, to decorate

SERVES 6

44

1 Peel, core and chop the apples. Place them in a saucepan with half the apple juice. Bring to the boil, then cover and simmer the apples gently until they are tender.

2 Purée the apples, with the honey and vanilla essence, in a blender or food processor. Spoon half the apple purée into a bowl and set it aside. Add half the blackberries to the remaining apple purée and process until smooth. Press the blackberry and apple purée through a sieve to remove the seeds.

3 Then pour the remaining apple juice into the clean pan and bring to just below boiling point. Sprinkle the gelatine over and stir until completely dissolved. Stir

half the gelatine into the plain apple purée and half into the blackberry and apple purée. Leave both purées to cool until they are on the verge of setting.

4 Whisk the egg whites until almost stiff, then fold them into the plain apple purée. Spoon half the mixture into a separate bowl. Stir in the remaining whole blackberries, then tip the mixture into a 1.75 litre/3 pint/7½ cup loaf tin, packing it down firmly. Top with the blackberry purée, spreading it level, then the remaining apple purée. Freeze the mixture until firm. Allow the terrine to soften slightly before serving it in slices, decorated with the fresh apple slices and the blackberries.

Iced Praline Torte

INGREDIENTS

115g/4oz/1 cup blanched almonds
120ml/4fl oz/½ cup water
350g/12oz/1½ cups caster sugar
115g/4oz/⅔ cup raisins
90ml/6 tbsp rum or brandy
115g/4oz dark chocolate, broken into squares
30ml/2 tbsp milk
475ml/16fl oz/2 cups double cream
30ml/2 tbsp strong black coffee
16 sponge fingers
DECORATION
150ml/¼ pint/⅔ cup double cream
50g/2oz/½ cup flaked almonds, toasted
15g/½ oz dark chocolate, melted

SERVES 8

1 Lightly grease a 1.2 litre/2 pint/5 cup loaf tin. Line with greaseproof paper or non-stick baking paper. Using the almonds, water and sugar, make and grind the praline, as for Praline Ice Cream. Tip the praline into a large mixing bowl and set aside.

2 Soak the raisins in half the rum or brandy for at least 1 hour. Melt the chocolate with the milk in a heatproof bowl over a pan of barely simmering water. Allow to cool.

3 Whip the double cream in a large mixing bowl until soft peaks form, then whisk in the chocolate. Fold in the praline and the soaked raisins, with any liquid.

4 Mix the coffee and the remaining rum or brandy in a shallow dish. Dip half the sponge fingers, one at a time, in the mixture, and arrange them in a layer over the bottom of the tin.

5 Cover with the chocolate mixture, then add another layer of dipped soaked sponge fingers. Cover the torte and freeze overnight.

6 Turn the frozen torte out on to a serving plate. Carefully remove the lining paper. Cover with the whipped cream, sprinkle the toasted almonds on top and drizzle the melted chocolate over. Serve in slices.

Black Forest Sundae

INGREDIENTS

400g/14oz can pitted black cherries in syrup
15ml/1 tbsp cornflour
45ml/3 tbsp kirsch
150ml/¼ pint/⅔ cup whipping cream
15ml/1 tbsp icing sugar
600ml/1 pint/2½ cups chocolate ice cream
115g/4oz chocolate cake, cut in large pieces
vanilla ice cream, to serve
8 fresh cherries, to decorate

SERVES 4

48

1 Strain the cherry syrup into a large saucepan, then spoon 30ml/2 tbsp of the syrup into a small bowl. Stir in the cornflour until the mixture is smooth.

2 Bring the syrup in the pan to the boil. Stir in the cornflour mixture, lower the heat and simmer briefly to thicken. Add the cherries, stir in the kirsch and spread the mixture out on a baking sheet to cool.

3 In a bowl, whip the cream with the icing sugar until soft peaks form. Place a spoonful of the cherry mixture in each of four sundae glasses. Top with layers of chocolate ice cream, pieces of chocolate cake, whipped cream and more cherry mixture, until the glasses are almost full.

4 Finish off each sundae with a final piece of chocolate cake, two scoops of ice cream and a whirl of fresh whipped cream. Decorate each with 2 fresh cherries and serve at once.

VARIATION

This particular sundae is based upon Black Forest Gateau, but you don't have to be tied to these ingredients. Invent your own combinations of fruit, ice cream, cake and cream.

Chocolate Mint Ice Cream Pie

INGREDIENTS

*75g / 3oz / ½ cup plain choolate, broken
into squares, or chocolate chips
40g / 1½oz / 3 tbsp butter
50g / 2oz / 2 cups crisped rice cereal
1 litre / 1¾ pints / 4 cups ready-made
mint-chocolate-chip ice cream, softened
until spreadable
75g / 3oz plain chocolate, in one piece*

SERVES 8

50

1 Line a 23cm/ 9in pie tin with foil, then add a second lining of non-stick baking paper. Melt the chocolate squares or chocolate chips with the butter in a heatproof bowl over barely simmering water. Remove from the heat and stir in the cereal, a little at a time. Cool for about 5 minutes.

2 Press the chocolate-coated cereal mixture evenly over the bottom and sides of the prepared tin, to make a pie shell with a 1cm/½in rim. Chill in the freezer until the cereal mixture has set completely.

3 Lift out the pie shell, then carefully peel away the paper and foil and return the shell to the tin. Spread the ice cream evenly into the pie shell, then freeze for about 1 hour, until firm.

4 Make the decoration. Soften the chocolate slightly by cupping it in your hands, then shave off short, wide curls with a swivel-bladed vegetable peeler. Scatter the curls over the ice cream pie just before serving.

Ice Cream Strawberry Shortcake

INGREDIENTS

3 x 15cm / 6in ready-made sponge cake cases
or shortcakes
1.2 litres / 2 pints / 5 cups vanilla or
strawberry ice cream, softened until spreadable
675g / 1½lb / 5 cups hulled strawberries,
halved if large
whipped cream, to serve (optional)

SERVES 4

1 If you are using sponge cake cases, trim off the raised edges with a sharp serrated knife. The sponge trimmings can be saved and used to make individual trifles.

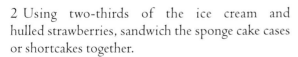

2 Using two-thirds of the ice cream and hulled strawberries, sandwich the sponge cake cases or shortcakes together.

3 Spoon the remaining ice cream on top, crown with the remaining strawberries. Serve the short-cake at once, with whipped cream, if liked.

COOK'S TIP
There is no neat way of cutting this delicious dessert. It will look glorious until you actually start to serve it, and that's what really matters.

Blackberry & Apple Romanoff

INGREDIENTS

4 sharp eating apples
45ml/3 tbsp caster sugar
250ml/8fl oz/1 cup whipping cream
5ml/1 tsp grated lemon rind
90ml/6 tbsp Greek-style yogurt
4–6 crisp meringues, roughly crumbled
225g/8oz/1½ cups fresh or thawed frozen blackberries
whipped cream, blackberries and fresh mint sprigs, to decorate

SERVES 6

52

2 Whip the cream with the remaining sugar in a large mixing bowl. Fold in the grated lemon rind and yogurt, then stir in the mashed apples and the meringues.

3 Gently stir in the blackberries, then tip all of the mixture into the pudding basin. Cover the basin with clear film and freeze for 1–3 hours, until the mixture is firm.

4 Turn out on to a chilled plate, lift off the clear film and pipe whipped cream around the base. Decorate with the blackberries and fresh mint sprigs.

1 Line a 900ml/ 1½ pint/4 cup pudding basin with clear film. Peel and core the apples, then slice them into a heavy-based frying pan. Add 30ml/2 tbsp

of the sugar. Cook the mixture for 2–3 minutes, or until the apples soften. Mash them with a fork and set the frying pan aside to cool.

Cranberry Bombe

INGREDIENTS

SORBET CENTRE
225g/8oz/2 cups fresh or frozen cranberries,
thawed if frozen, plus extra to decorate
150ml/¼ pint/⅔ cup orange juice
finely grated rind of ½ orange
½ tsp allspice
50g/2oz/⅓ cup raw sugar
OUTER LAYER
1 quantity Vanilla Ice Cream
1oz/2 tbsp chopped angelica
1oz/2 tbsp mixed peel
½oz/1 tbsp flaked almonds, toasted

SERVES 6

54

1 Line a 1.2 litre/ 2 pint/5 cup pudding basin with clear film. Make the sorbet centre. Put the cranberries, orange juice, rind and spice in a saucepan. Cook  gently until the cranberries are soft. Stir in the sugar, then purée the mixture in a food processor until almost smooth, but with some texture. Set the saucepan aside to cool.

2 Allow the Vanilla Ice Cream to soften slightly, then tip it into a bowl and stir in the chopped angelica, mixed peel and flaked almonds.

3 Pack the mixture into the prepared pudding basin and use the back of a dessert spoon to hollow out the centre. Cover and freeze until firm.

4 Fill the hollow in the ice cream with the cranberry mixture. Freeze again until firm. When ready to serve, invert the bombe on a chilled plate and  lift off the clear film. Allow the bombe to soften slightly at room temperature before serving it in slices, decorated with fresh cranberries.

COOK'S TIP
This luxurious iced dessert tastes great on hot summer evenings but it also makes a wonderful alternative to Christmas Pudding. It is easy to make, popular with children and requires absolutely no attention on the day!

Iced Drinks

Café Glacé

INGREDIENTS

600ml / 1 pint / 2½ cups water
30–45ml / 2–3 tbsp instant coffee granules
15ml / 1 tbsp caster sugar
600ml / 1 pint / 2½ cups milk
6 ice cubes
12 scoops of vanilla ice cream
6 chocolate flakes, to decorate
12 crisp dessert biscuits, to serve

SERVES 6

1 Bring 120ml/ 4floz/½ cup of the water to the boil, pour into a small bowl and stir in the coffee. Stir in the sugar until dissolved. Leave to cool, then chill for about 2 hours.

2 Mix the milk and remaining water in a large jug. Add the chilled coffee mixture and mix well. Divide the mixture among six brandy snifters or cocktail glasses, filling them three-quarters full.

3 Add an ice cube and 2 scoops of vanilla ice cream to each glass. Decorate with the chocolate flakes and serve with the biscuits.

Coffee Granita

INGREDIENTS

115g/4oz/½ cup granulated sugar
475ml/16fl oz/2 cups water
250ml/8fl oz/1 cup very strong black
coffee, cooled
dessert biscuits, to serve
DECORATION
250ml/8fl oz/1 cup double cream, whipped
with 10ml/2 tsp icing sugar

SERVES 4

58

1 Mix the sugar and water in a saucepan. Stir over a low heat until the sugar dissolves, then boil, without stirring, for about 2 minutes. Remove from the heat and allow to cool.

2 Add the coffee to the sugar syrup in the saucepan and mix together. Then pour the mixture into a shallow freezer tray and freeze for several hours until it is solid.

3 To remove from the freezer tray, plunge the bottom of the container into very hot water for a few seconds, then turn out the frozen coffee mixture and chop it into large chunks.

4 Place the frozen coffee chunks in a food processor and process until the ice breaks down to a mass of small crystals. Spoon into tall serving glasses and top each glass with a spoonful of the sweetened whipped cream.

COOK'S TIP

If you do not wish to serve the granita immediately, pour the processed mixture back into the freezer tray and freeze until serving time. Thaw for a few minutes before serving, or process again.

Iced Mint & Chocolate Cooler

INGREDIENTS

60ml/4 tbsp drinking chocolate
400ml/14fl oz/1¾ cups chilled milk
150ml/¼ pint/⅔ cup natural yogurt
2.5ml/½ tsp peppermint essence
4 scoops of chocolate ice cream
mint leaves and chocolate shapes, to decorate

SERVES 4

60

2 Pour the liquid into a large mixing bowl or large jug and whisk in the remaining milk. Then, add the natural yogurt and the peppermint essence to the jug.

3 Pour the mixture into four tall glasses and top each with a scoop of chocolate ice cream. Decorate each of the glasses with the fresh mint leaves and assorted chocolate shapes. Serve immediately.

1 Place the drinking chocolate in a small saucepan and stir in about 120ml/4fl oz/ ½ cup of chilled milk. Gently heat the liquid, stirring constantly, until almost boiling, then remove the saucepan from the heat and allow the liquid to cool.

COOK'S TIP
Cocoa powder can be used instead of drinking chocolate, if preferred, but remember that cocoa can be quite bitter: you may need to add sugar to taste.

Blushing Piña Colada

INGREDIENTS

1 banana
1 thick slice of pineapple
75ml / 5 tbsp pineapple juice
1 scoop strawberry ice cream or sorbet
25ml / 1½ tbsp coconut milk
1 small scoop finely crushed ice (see Cook's Tip)
30ml / 2 tbsp grenadine
stemmed maraschino cherries, to decorate

SERVES 2

1 Peel the banana and chop it roughly. Cut two small wedges from the pineapple and set aside for the decoration. Then peel and chop the remaining pine-

apple and add it to the blender with the banana and pineapple juice. Process to a smooth purée.

2 Add the strawberry ice cream or sorbet to the blender. Pour in the coconut milk and add the scoop of finely crushed ice. Process until smooth.

3 Then divide the drink between two large, well-chilled glasses. Trickle the grenadine syrup over the top of the piña colada; it will filter through the drink to give a pink blush effect.

4 Slit the reserved pineapple wedges, and slip one on to the rim of each glass. Then add a maraschino cherry in the same way. Serve the blushing piña colada with drinking straws.

COOK'S TIP
Never try to crush ice in a blender;
it will ruin the blades. Put the ice cubes in a
strong plastic bag and crush them finely with
a rolling pin before adding to the blender.

62

Index